Phantasmal Flowers in The Eden Where Only I Know

YUU IKEDA

Published by Black Sunflowers Poetry Press
www.blacksunflowerspoetry.com

© Yuu Ikeda 2023
ISBN: 978-1-7396267-4-7
All rights reserved

Contents

flower	1
FloweR	2
fLOwer	3
floWeR	4
FLOweR	5
fLoWER	6
flOwEr	7
FlOwEr	8
FLOWer	9
flOWeR	10
floweR	11
FLOWeR	12
fLower	13
floWer	14
flowEr	15
FloWER	16
FlOwer	17
fLoweR	18
FloWeR	19
floWEr	20
FloWEr	21
FlowER	22
fLOWer	23
fLOWER	24
fLoWeR	25
FLoWEr	26
FLOWER	27

flower

Guilty spring breeze
caresses
cheeks of the flower.

The flower never cries.
The flower never smiles.

Blood-orange petals
stone-cold
in sparse sunlight.
The pale face
resigned
because of spring.

FloweR

Scent allows me
to imagine a hopeful future.
And,
scent takes hopeless reality
away from me.

The scent is remedy.
The scent is a drug.
The scent is atonement.
The scent is repentance.

fLOwer

only i know
you are crying
under the inhumane sun.

only i know
you are smiling
under silky rain.

when everyone looks up at the sun,
you and i feel something
like an icy blanket.
when everyone escapes from the rain,
you are i feel something
like a warm diamond.

floWeR

Moonlit skin
reflects bloodless emotion.
Whenever this world is drunk on vice,
blood rushes
but controls every emotion.

FLOweR

Memories of dawn
dye the petals.

So, you are beautiful.

Memories of midnight
cling to the stem.

So, you are mysterious.

fLoWER

She has no past.
But what she has is
—the phantasmal future—
where everything hugs her
and welcomes her all.

flOwEr

Time is never etched on the face.
The flower is just alive,
wanting water and rejecting water.
Time never allows the flower
to etch something on the face.
Only sunlight makes her feel that
she is just alive.

FlOwEr

why am I blooming
yet no one sees me?
why am I smiling
yet nothing flows into me?
why am I gazing at the sun
yet I can't touch
the surface of passion?

FLOWer

when she lost the way
to bloom free~~ly~~,
water to live
changed to
a knife to feed death.

flOWeR

The moon whispers to darkness that
the flower is breathing.

As Cupid kisses Psyche's lips,
the moon cocoons the flower
in a ray of vulnerable light.

As Psyche answers to the Cupid's kiss,
the flower quivers.

floweR

The morning glow
shines on me
telling of
spring melodies
beginning to float
throughout the poetic world.

Leaves applaud,
tiny birds sing,
dewdrops ascend
to the pastel sky.

I'm swaying,
feeling the beginning of every prayer.

FLOWeR

Blue wind moistens my dry passion.
In the misty night,
the flame I lost
again blooms
on the ground where I stand.
A step to the fire
makes way to freedom.

fLower

Petals of the sun
burn,
lest she forgets, eyes of love.

Wrapped in the blanket,
she stands at
the edge of the road.

Even when she can't feel water,
the warmth gives her silky hopes to live.
She never wilts,
    — she knows love.

floWer

pain is evidence.
memories are drugs.
and water to live by, withers my days.

flowEr

Falling snowdrops soak into my veins

Umbrella of sunlight breaks,
Shroud of clouds spreads its wings.

A gray city looks down on me.
Dead me looks down on fragments of
everlasting winter.

FloWER

can you live without feeling normal?
can you live, feeling madness?
can you live without the proof that
you are a human?
can you live with the proof that
you are not a human?

FlOwer

I can't attract butterflies.
My petals smell like sin.
My petals look like a devil.
Every butterfly escapes my shadow.
I look down into a puddle
reflecting misery.

fLoweR

Love is the sole rope
that I cling to.
Whenever cherry blossoms bloom,
I cling.
Even when I know that it is an apparition,
I cling.
Behind cherry blossoms,
I also bloom,
hoping the solitary rope holds true.

FloWeR

Running mind
never dyes the petals
passionate red that she wants most.
Only her mind -runs
on the invisible road.
Only tears flow
from her dull eyes.

floWEr

my first dance was in the morning glow,
with spring breeze.
petals emitted a ray of hope.
the horizon dyed in a faint orange
celebrated us.
my first dance was in the morning glow,
with spring breeze.
from that time,
my days started in a true sense.

FloWEr

Rain of guilt drops on me.
icicles on a cold day.
stains of coffee
on a favorite blanket.
Rain of guilt wets my eyelids
unless I open my eyes completely.

FlowER

A plant of ridicule is blooming
beside me.
Whenever wind blows,
the plant sways and smiles, silently,
as though a devil pierces my veins.
Whenever the sun shines,
the plant looks up and smiles silently,
as though an angel saps my veins.

fLOWer

What is this thirst?

I drink so much water.
But I'm always thirsty.

What is this thirst?

I have many hopes.
But I'm always thirsty.

fLOWER

The call to the future
hastens me.
The blinking candles;
not only my energy
but my resignation.

fLoWeR

Powder snow leads me
to a road of atonement.
Woeful clouds spread arms,
hug my torment
—dying the world holy white.

FLoWEr

The rhythm of summer
does her dance passionately.
Sprouts of dreams
begin a hopeful song
at her base
The oath to dreams
begins to whirl
below.

FLOWER

The last flower
leaves every hope
to spring.

Being dyed pastel pink,
the last flower closes its eyes.

'Even if my eyes can't see your eyes,
every inch of me feels your breath.
Even if my brain can't reflect your silhouette,
every inch of me resounds with
your heartbeats.

Black Sunflowers Poetry Press, 2023

www.ingramcontent.com/pod-product-compliance
Lightning Source LLC
Chambersburg PA
CBHW042131100526
44587CB00026B/4255